PAST IMPERFECT

PAST IMPERFECT **SUZANNE BUFFAM** POEMS

ANANSI

Published in 2005 by
House of Anansi Press Inc.
110 Spadina Avenue, Suite 801
Toronto, ON, M5V 2K4
Tel. 416-363-4343
Fax 416-363-1017
www.anansi.ca

Distributed in Canada by
HarperCollins Canada Ltd.
1995 Markham Road
Scarborough, ON, M1B 5M8
Toll free tel. 1-800-387-0117

Distributed in the United States by
Publishers Group West
1700 Fourth Street
Berkeley, CA 94710
Toll free tel. 1-800-788-3123

Permission is gratefully acknowledged to reproduce the following:
(front-cover photograph) Anne Wilson, Eat.205, 2004.
Still from *Errant Behaviors*, a video/sound installation
(composer: Shawn Decker; animator: Cat Solen; post-production animator
and mastering: Daniel Torrente). Copyright © 2004 Anne Wilson.

House of Anansi Press is committed to protecting our natural environment.
As part of our efforts, this book is printed on Rolland Enviro paper: it contains
100% post-consumer recycled fibres, is acid-free, and is processed chlorine-free.

09 08 07 06 05   2 3 4 5 6

LIBRARY AND ARCHIVES CANADA CATALOGUING IN PUBLICATION DATA

Buffam, Suzanne, 1972–
Past imperfect / Suzanne Buffam.

Poems.
ISBN 0-88784-726-9

I. Title.

PS8603.U44P38 2005   C811'.6   C2005-900647-1

Cover design: Bill Douglas at The Bang
Front-cover photograph: Anne Wilson
Author photograph: Ann Buffam
Typesetting: Brian Panhuyzen

Canada Council   Conseil des Arts
for the Arts   du Canada

ONTARIO ARTS COUNCIL
CONSEIL DES ARTS DE L'ONTARIO

*We acknowledge for their financial support of our publishing program the
Canada Council for the Arts, the Ontario Arts Council, and the Government of
Canada through the Book Publishing Industry Development Program (BPIDP).*

Printed and bound in Canada

For Chicu

CONTENTS

I

II

'Twas best imperfect — as it was —

— Emily Dickinson, 696

I

ANOTHER BILDUNGSROMAN

I grow up and leave home.
Fall in all kinds of love, none the wiser.
Now it's time, as they say, to move forward.
I gather all the loose change in the house,
find I have amassed a small fortune.
At the bank, waiting to speak with a teller,
I read a pamphlet that informs me
how much larger my small fortune
could have been by now if only.
I decide, instead, to go to France.
I take a little room on the Rue de Seine,
get lost at Versailles, fail to befriend
the handsome waiter at the Café Crème.
When I get back it's late fall, the pool
in the park is locked up, clogged with leaves.
Squirrels, hard-wired for the future,
are burying nuts in the threadbare lawn.
Wind comes down the mountain with a rose in its teeth.
There are gaps in the sky the sky fills in with sky.

LACRIMAE RERUM

I have a friend who believes, if not in the actual merging of souls, at least in the value of this fiction. Another subscribes to the notion we are constantly reborn, over and over, until we have endured every possible form of existence on earth. Such theories of the soul are like thin, fraying ropes across a vast, airy chasm through which a bittersweet wind forever blows. On one side, sheep grazing a meadow of clover and moss. On the other side, mutton and wool socks for all.

•

Kamikaze pilots are taught to remember, when diving into the enemy, to shout at the top of their lungs: *Hissatsu!* Sink without fail! At that moment, the handbook assures, all the cherry blossoms at Yasukuni shrine will smile brightly on you.

•

Look more closely from farther away. That is my way of thinking, writes the amateur astronomer Tsuruhiko Kiuchi, upon leaving the Japanese airforce to serve the night sky from below, which, he believes, is like searching for yourself.

•

In Peekskill, New York, on the evening of October 9, 1992, football fans observe a large fireball breaking up in the sky above the field. They watch it pass before the moon and split into hundreds of brilliant, green shards, one of which descends on the parking lot and crashes through the roof of a Buick.

•

The first time I kiss a boy with my tongue I go home and copy out our names, over and over on the back of a book, until the words become beautiful sounds. Not until he forgets my name two weeks later at a high-school dance, under streetlights and cosmic debris, do I understand the failure of language.

SIR GROMORE SOMYR JOURE

That was a happy station, full of sunshine and cabbage.
You could sit among the thinkers for hours,
thinking anything you wanted. You could think
about your kingdom and feel a small stab of remorse,
or you could cultivate an interest in the funnel-shaped
webs leading down through the grasswort
towards what toothed and cruel centre lay waiting.
Knees were for kneeling. Lashes were for looking
at the sun. The river was slow and it hurried.
Trains slowed down but did not stop.
Wherefore was the question on everyone's lips
though none spoke it, nor plucked it away
but let it hang there like an overripe pear
left out for the gleaners to dispute in the fall.
Every horse had three different names, each one
more purple than the last. Sir Gromore Somyr Joure
took the day every day until the very day
he retired. Did I love that dark horse?
I did not. His breath stank of cabbage.
He bit the hands that fed him. He would stand
in bad weather and refuse the boxwood gate.
But I was there in the fray and the fanfare,
I was there in the dooryard, and I was there
when they laid him down cold to the earth.

IN WHICH ALL WILL BE REVEALED

They've found another moon around Jupiter.
News of this reaches me too late
to get out of bed and arrest it
with my bloodshot and glowering eyes.
Instead I will just lie here in my slippers
and listen to the hourly reports.
Also, I will listen to the sound of my teeth
which is how I imagine the earth would sound
if you could press an ear to the dirt
and hear the heavy plates grinding in their sleep.
What, in the final analysis, isn't imminent?
Or, for that matter, immanent?
Even my lumps have lumps.
My lovers, lovers.

MY ESCAPE

Some people were dancing under a large silver ball. Others were just standing around, swaying a bit, opening and closing their mouths like fish in a bowl. I could see I had made a grave mistake. I feared I would have to explain myself, but the coat-check girl just took my stub and handed over my jacket with a drowsy smile. For this I had travelled over mountains? For this I had swallowed a river of salt? A boy walked by with a glass of champagne full of bubbles the same shade of pink as my toenails. I thought, "He will come back now. He will offer you a taste of those bubbles and it will be the first taste." I thought, "The rivers and mountains are a story you can reread at leisure, or put back on the shelf and forget." I thought, "Now you will never disappear." The moment came and went in a cloud of dry ice. I found a side door behind a large potted palm and slipped out. Outside it was quiet. The sky was far away. I could see dark shapes in a nearby field. People were dancing under a large silver ball.

AND ALSO THE PLEIADES

I go outside and look up. The moon has sunk below the rooftops in the west, dragging her wet skirts behind her. It is one thing to call it a dark sky in winter, another entirely to erase the painted moon and stars. Even standing very still like this is a kind of white lie. There is how I feel, and there is this hurtling surface. It is impossible to say something true for all time about either. I look at the rooftops. I look at the dark little chimney pots. I look at the snow that does not glitter where it lands. And no I am not thinking of you either, not remembering a certain bright shape moving smoothly towards and away.

DEAR FUTURE

Among the quay's sundry distractions today
is a man practicing scales by the houseboats.
On a small, silver trumpet he climbs
up the notes and then down, the descent

no less difficult for having been travelled.
Perhaps he has come here to placate
his neighbours. The notes come out pinched
and off-kilter, small, stubborn slivers

the morning refuses. Behind him the swallows
climb and drop through the minutes, scoring
the river, the opposite bank, and the poplars:
they ride out to the edge of each octave and stall

before dropping back down to the river's
own endless inflection. But oh, the young man
is improving. Can you hear him approach?
He must learn each note so well he can forget it.

PLAY

He has put his shirt on backwards and allowed her,
just this once, to touch his face. Her arms
reach through the empty sleeves and in

this game, they've become his. His hands
hang empty at his sides. They share the body
of one child. The mirror gives back one body

of two minds. One sees the other's fingers
find his eyes and knows to hold them closed
until she's finished with the lids. Because

she's seen it done before, she knows to still
the chin while filling in the other's lips, although,
this time, she's working blind. She stills him

with a finger and he feels his own chin quiver
when she laughs. And since she can't see
where she's been, the colour thickens in some places

and in others doesn't take. They name this face.
They dream up something ugly and it sticks.

HOUSE

We've found a hospital. The sick are missing
limbs, eyes, buttons, pins, and have been welcomed
for today back to the game.

They wait all day to see the doctor,
propped against the mantelpiece, above
the tinderbox that has been turned

into a gurney for a child, overlooked
while we look for the clock. We are not
interested in plot. Our pleasure's

in the furniture, a rearranging of the rooms
inside the head. The doctor waits
to see the lady with the nickname

appliquéd across the bodice of her spangled
fitted dress. He'll wait all day.
No one decided this. We simply

know it as we did not know
before we opened it — before it
opened us. There is a room inside the room

inside the room we find by wanting
it, in which a single, unplugged lamp
stands in for light.

THERE GOES A WINDOW

Someone is smashing up the house next door.
Smashing its eyes out, smashing up
its coffers, its lintels, and its delicate, filigreed lid.
But it's okay — there's a sign out front

that says so. Getting paid to do a job
makes it legitimate and brings the sun out
from behind a black cloud. No one
is paying me to say this. My kitchen,

as it happens, is in fact full of crumbs.
I have a wealth of rare books in my closet,
and a dearth of understanding in my heart.
Last night I saw an astral light

through a copse of black trees in the distance.
Others stood with me on the close-cropped lawn.
I heard one say the word *glomerulus*,
which I learned has to do with the spleen.

Or the kidneys, the coccyx, or the peace
which surpasseth all thought. There was dew
on our feet. We went on sipping
from our drinks. Then a mosquito

landed gently on my wrist and without
warning, withdrew from me
a priceless draught of my life's major work.
I don't know how else to put it.
To speak at all is to speak in tongues.

OPEN WATER

In the dream I have been fatally wounded
by a shark and wake up to discover
I have only been seriously maimed.
Another piece of good news
is delivered in the form of a tiny green bug
that circles my head and flies off
in the general direction of spring.
I vow then and there to take action, before
it takes me. The morning gives back
my face, wide-eyed and bulbous, swimming
upside-down in the bowl of my spoon.
I build a raft in the basement out of blankets and string.
My friends all think I'm in Texas,
which, in a way, I am.

BEST-CASE SCENARIO

At second glance the leaves are bright green
and the dog is asleep. The omelette slides

from the pan intact. No one we know
serves us tea. It is sweet. It tastes faintly

exotic but also sad, like the jasmine blossoms
wilting in our hair. High, high above,

clouds grind light into dust-motes.
Because we have not died yet of hope,

nor its opposite, we remain here among
these creaturely feelings, indentured

to the small brown birds that will not
light on our hair. So be it. Our shadows

on the grass may be luckier, although
their fate is such that they won't know it.

HAPPINESS IS NOT THE ONLY HAPPINESS

My hair has grown well past my shoulders,
a feat I achieved by not cutting it.

Also this year I have learned something new
about daylight. It keeps us awake.

Likewise the moonlight, the searchlight,
the low blue glow on the dashboard

that carries each through her own private dark.
Rue is a sun-loving plant.

Tornadoes *want* us to chase them.
When summer finally arrives it arrives

in a rainstorm. Wind enters the spruce
and comes out wearing sparrows.

Some say water tastes best
from a bucket, some say a cupped palm.

TWO HANDS

One hand flashes a mirror at the sun.
The other casts the shadow of a wing.

•

One hand opens a window.
The other hand lowers a lid.

•

One hand holds a nail.
The other hand loses the hammer in the grass.

•

One hand wears a ring.
One wears a scar where a ring used to be.

•

One hand tears up a note.
The other hand tapes back the petals on a rose.

•

One sifts through a box of old photographs for the boy
  half-buried in sand.
One hangs the empty frame back on its hook.

●

One wrenches a nest from the crook of a branch.
One finds enough dropped feathers to build a whole bird.

●

One builds a box.
One buries the bird on the ridge.

●

One locks up the cabin.
One turns back the hands of a clock.

●

One grips the railing.
One drops a silver chain into the lake.

●

One presses a small yellow bud between the chapter on
   love and the chapter on desire without an object.
One leaves the book out in the rain.

●

One hand tests the waters.
The other hand traces a name across the waves.

BEFORE DARKNESS

Empty, the dresses in the window are more beautiful.
In a stillness between thinking she remembers
thinking: if not waiting, what then?
Before darkness, after sunset, there's a window
in the day through which light passes, without
shadow, and shadow simply happens
where nothing blocks the light. The dresses
in this window wear a stillness
she thought to call its opposite.
Now she revises: she wants
to touch them. They want not to be touched.

II

THE GARDEN (I)

How the winged ants and the honeybees,
large and dark as human eyes, the butterfly
clapping its wings on the branch like a bat,
the heather, the mint, the bronchial
grapes and the maple

cohere. How simple
the garden, in its lucid confusion, the mind
in the plummet of sleep: no need
to remember, no need to forget —
just the hum and buzz of the world,

begetting. As though by paying close enough
attention to the garden I might
join it. As though I might relinquish
this slavish devotion and begin,
at last, to mean something, the way

the wasp, waist-deep, headlong
inside a bitter grape
means business. There is no simple way
to say this. I am simply
abuzz with instincts

I cannot comprehend. And my head
gets in the way of everything, the way the house
gets in the way of everything outside.

THE STARFISH

A wave reached up to tug my hem.
Because of you I let it pull me in.
And then I turned from where you stood
delighting in my own delight at yours
in my soaked skirt, and swam towards
the middle of the lake. Between my strokes,
erratic, slack, small buffetings
that gave the day, your laughter
from the shore, their shape. Your skipped
voice lit across the waves and gave me
something vanishing to aim for, something solid
to outreach. Did I want you to lose sight of me?
Just long enough for me to learn
how being lost would feel? I felt your watching
for my face, my wave, for any solid part
of what I'd led you to believe. I leaned
back in the lake and let it take me, almost,
under. Above my waist, fanned out around me
in the waves, my skirt rose up and made of me
a shape I couldn't take on shore or keep.

LIFE WITH FOLDED UMBRELLA

Neither rain nor shine for days
and days and everywhere the grey
grains linger on the still-

green fidgetings of things not yet
reclaimed. All summer we sat
in its generous shade, and watched

the plot we'd planted come
into its own slow going.
We didn't think

to thank it for its role, so deftly
and discreetly played out on the bare
stage of the deck. Now the wide

white canvas canopy
is folded on its pole. I sit
behind the windows and consider

how it fits into the simple triptych
of their frames: set off
a little to the left, and taller than

the staggered aspens in the background,
and beyond, along the ridge
of cordgrass and blue asters

on the slip of island that divides
the glassy saltmarsh from the tides,
the shaggy shelvings of the pines

— now ponderous and drab, now
springing swiftly into business
with a sudden lift in wind —

it nearly fills the centre pane.
It makes a simple shape
against the grains, now furrowed

like the folds of snow-draped
fields, where what you see
is not so much the story

going forward, as the space
the story clears
for what comes next.

THE WASP

It hovers at the basin's lip — a wish
to enter and a wall, invisible,

that stops it. The soapy water must be sweet
enough to coax it to the edge but not

enough to draw it, fully, in.
Slim panelled wings glint quicker

than the glimpse. Why doesn't it drink?
The wall must be an answer to its will.

Madder in amber, blebbed glass, intention
caught on the edge of an act — the small

body blurs in the light. Oh I can tell
it wants in. I can tell by the way it resists.

INKLINGS

I

Where use comes to ruin
begins beauty —

rooms once thick with fruit
grown unruly

have outstripped their function
to stand in a pasture

collapsing. Here you stray
towards grace. Here you

stumble the mud-runnelled
hallways while off-

stage the escapes
take the acre.

II

God is waiting, you say
to nobody's face —

to the stains on the river
some hunters created

one daybreak, their names
now all but dissolved

on the grey slates I want not
to wonder — so wander

all over its face —

III

Not a hole in the sky
for my eye

to climb up through
this morning. No window

of you. Not an inkling
of elsewhere

to stare myself into.
Just wind

from the west
spreading silver

down over this rock
-riddled distance

these inches I wish
nonetheless

to have entered.

IV

Given a gap
for these visions to land in

and linger, we dressed them
in rags of bright satin, believing

whatever we clothed
could be cloistered. Still

the voice slips free
from the singer. The cloak slips

from the last blackbird's shoulders
as it lifts from its perch

on the polefence and feathers
out over the open

no single perspective
can measure. Were we meant

to retrieve it you'd think
we'd be gifted with less.

V

It starts in the scrub brush —
one waxwing

calls in my coming — it catches
and soon it has spread

to the candling branches
upriver — downwind

of this false spark of spring.
No wonder

so sudden. No wonder
so fit to be kindled.

So the touch
of another sends ripples

long after its
sting is extinguished. So

late winter blazes. When
the last fruits are stripped

it will lift.

VI

I was lucky enough.
I lived for a while

between barrens
and shared my crust

for a time without upset.
Nothing wasn't. It

wasn't enough. When you
covered my eyes I was nothing

but hush in the unnumbered
rushes, undone.

It was something. *It was.*

VII

Let three sunlit minutes
on this ridge equal

bliss. Let bliss
be quick. Let it slip

through the rips
in the runnels above us.

Enough
to have lived

without touching one
inch. Let the sting

of my wishing
you with me

be swift.

PROJECT

A bridge, lifted
out of the mist,
resurrected

first in the mind,
in the pure world
of idea, lifted

with longing, lifted
with praise — the intricate
arches, interlocked

timbers, even-beamed
ballast. Praise
the joinings.

Praise the brushwork.
Will it hold them?
Will it hold up under

hurry, delay, a pair
of bulls led by rings
through the nose towards

market? The future?
I drop a stone
and hear it open

a hole in the river
where current will carry it
— sifting the stone

through its fingers
and turning it over
and over towards where

it won't stay.

STONES

Think of a tall glass of water.
Think of it on a table
in a panel of sunlight.

Think of the small bubbles rushing
to marry the sunlight,
bursting with hurry.

Think of the column of buttons
done up in a hurry
along the small bones of the back.

And the trail of footsteps
that doesn't turn back,
leading down to the harbour

where three buoys mark
the blue of the harbour
turning into the blue of the distance.

Think of a woman
staring off in the distance
while she worries the stones

at her throat. Now hear it breaking,
the rain of dark stones
striking the floor at her feet.

THE BRIDGE

A strong wind corrugates the surface.
Eddies collect and sip at the edges.
Light splits and scatters all component parts.
The bright blue scales slap up.
Particles of ash, particles of history
drift in from the distance.
I stand on the bridge looking down.
                                    An equal
and opposite force presses back — burning
leaves, steaming tarmac, fallen twigs lifted
and ferried downstream, met by the wind's
swift resistance, your voice
in my ear breathing *foxglove*.

MEANWHILE

But could not keep so let seep in the wind.
So rolled the windows down and let it roar.
So felt the fingerbones inside me find
the fingered thing inside this foreign core.

So thickened by the inches, minutes, and the miles,
it hurled us into onwards and so through
the wet blue rolling landscape meanwhile's
made of where we're quickened and most true.

So made of us a place we can return to
when we're far. We are. We're far
from where we've been so far and who. It's you —

It's you to whom I'm speaking now so far
from you with whom I'll lie down when we're through.
So loosed the breathing we inside we are.

THE GARDEN (II)

When she does not think about him, very likely
she is thinking: "How the winged ants
and the honeybees," "How simple," "the way
the wasp, waist-deep, headlong

inside a bitter grape." Very likely she is counting
to a hundred, while the garden
goes about its humming like a dizzy field of atoms
she can't enter. She may

have an end in mind, and not yet know it,
or else she knows it all too well and yet is willing
— and is *working* — to deny it.
Very likely she is hoping

to forget him, the way the wind,
at rest above the garden, will forget
— without forsaking it —
to scuff the glassy surface of the pond.

POSTSCRIPT

There is a bridge across the river
built entirely of light.

Here swallows thread the middle distance
insects quicken with delight.

Delight because I say it is, because
it might be nothing but their hunger

buzzing dully into less. I sit among
the reeds. I read your note.

On the far shore now a carnival begins
to spin its burning wheel —

III

PLEASE TAKE BACK THE SPARROWS

Please take back the sparrows. They are bothersome and
cute. They are brown and daily all year long. They make
a plaything of the wind and the spruce. They come too
close. They look right at me with their tiny black eyes.
They dart through spaces. They pick up the pieces and
the pace. From rooftop to eavestrough to wire to branch
— they spring spring spring spring spring spring spring.
They are not sorry. They are not singing. Many they are
one they are never not somewhere. They are not not
singing. They are not slack. They fear the blue jay and the
airedale. They drink from the pond! They scatter think-
ing. They are not asking or telling they are scattering
thinking they are shivering. They are awake or they are
shivering. Please, take back the sparrows. They bathe in
dust.

WRONG NUMBERS

Flying through the half-built house,
arms akimbo, feet working the pedals
of the clumsy machine your body's become,

nosing up just in time to clear the treacherous sill
— then waking again in your childhood bed,
glimpsing an edge of the sea

through fluttering drapes, or maybe a secret
game of croquet on the snow-covered lawn,
you feel something crucial has been recovered,

maybe a loss. It hangs in the air all day
like spring rain. It hangs in your eyes all day
like a haze. You get carried away

with a pair of blunt scissors and suddenly,
there you are, staring down at a sink full of bangs.
There you are checking your ankles for wings.

The sky just doesn't spring back like it used to.
The house tilts more and more to the west every day.
Who can keep up? Not the dead in their drawers

on the hillside, not the mailman stuffing the slot
with an urgent mess addressed to the previous tenant.
The facts keep changing, but the number of facts

stays the same. By mid-morning the oil drum is empty,
the sun has replaced the buckle on Orion's silver belt.
It's colder and brighter than ever, and even the birds

give off steam, stationed in the poplar
like frets on the neck of a rustic guitar.
After all those years of practice, surely the wind

could pick out a more musical tune. But your heart
hums along. The heavens, you read,
are a mist of dust and gas. You show

the dentist where it hurts
and he removes it.

SHAPES AT MIDNIGHT

Across the street the artists are still working in their studios.
Through my curtains I can see them, moving now towards,
now away from the assorted shapes and colours
on the walls, each private artist vibrant in her cell.

On the second floor, a woman reaches out
as though to grasp a wedge of blue and reposition it,
  a careful
movement, full of a new love of ideas and distrust
of the heart. At the last second, before her hand connects

up with the colour and commits, she draws it back
and stands there, in the centre of her life, lit starkly
by the swinging bulb above her. Hoisted in the branches
of the maple is the moon

that dropped behind the poplars last November, when you
first introduced me to this version of despair: halfway
we cannot bear yet here
we long to stay: the artists in their studios, the sentimental

rectangles of blue, the moon, the ramifying
branches of the maple through the window,
halfway between the woman I am watching
and myself, beginning at this hour to lose green.

WHAT IS CALLED DÉJÀ VU

Rain taps little circles in the pavement that glisten, briefly,
then vanish. Your fingers
tap along my spine.
A slant wind. Eavestroughs.

Far off, the sound of a train
forging into its whistle unspools
a wake of old longings. The box
opens in on itself

like a dream inside which a crouched
animal is awaiting
release, recognition.
Its little teeth glisten.

SWEET BASIL

To make them last, I planted them in sunlight
in a half-filled drinking glass.
This way, according to a friend, they'll stay
what we call *good*
for days. Which means, I guess, stay green — and
  maybe even

grow a bit
before the smallest, topmost leaves
give in, at last, to letting go (of what? go where? Go *bad*
  we say
when we don't know . . . the body going off
somewhere we can't

yet follow, not yet
gone, and us, still not quite ready to have
done with it, no longer able to make
use . . .). And yes, it seems
this *is* the way: late afternoon, day two, and still

these stiff twin tongues
unfurl from every seam, as if the broken
body's news has yet to reach them
from below. How can't
they know? Or do they simply

disagree? I keep a photo of myself, at twelve, just then
beginning to grow proud — my body
among cousins in the bathtub, facing straight
into the future. The water cuts us
at the waist. Regardless

of its government, these slender
tendrils keep on drinking in
a kind of after-half-life in this glass,
where light above, and light below
meet halfway up the stem.

THE ONSET

Farewell to insects, farewell
to the numerous finches,
to wandering coatless
under the palm-sized
leaves of the maple.

Turn up your collar, sharpen
your intellect, prepare
again for hunger.
If only the body
could make up its mind.

If only the river
flowed one way —
but there goes a bottle,
caught on the chop
of a wave pushing north

back into current
while the depths plough south
towards candour.
In winter the river
will lock. Too late, too late

the wind in the branches
will chant, but today —
bright aberration, brief check
in the chain leading up to
decision — the wind

is lifting the fallen leaves back to the trees.

COMPANY

There is nothing to turn to.

There is an opening.

Beauty inquires within.

How long have you lived here?

Are you happy?

You answer each question

by repeating it, until its edges loosen.

A man walks by with a small dog wearing a sweater.

You are both more and less

alone than you thought.

IN BROAD DAYLIGHT

It was snowing and then it was Snowing.
I pictured small drops falling
mindless and radiant, self-contained lakes
hitting the cold and transforming
into filigreed stars, no two alike.
All over town, people were opening and closing doors.
It was Tuesday.
It was my birthday.
Rather, it was *as if* it were my birthday
and people in the park were laughing in French.
That's how simple it was. Then I knew
I had only to close my eyes and lie down there
on the star-covered bench, and nothing
at all would happen, which would be nearly enough.

IN WHICH I AM ATTACKED

I thought it was spring
and went out without my hat, without
my hatchet. Wrong again. It was fall
and the swans were eyeing me coldly
from the centre of the lake,
preparing to wound me again
with the sight of their beautiful backs.
A little boy ran up
and pulled my hair and ran off.
For months you're a smudge on the rug,
watching the wind blow, maybe taking
your pulse every hour or so, and then
all of a sudden, you're It.

IN WHICH I TAKE A DEEP BREATH

and let it out slowly
so that it leaves my body like a long white train
pulling out of the station
on the platform of which
I am standing
with one hand to my brow
and one hand waving
in the manner of a tired queen
at the tail of a great procession
through all the green and crowded
alleys of my childhood
grateful for the tiny silver hatpins
that keep everything in place

ANAKTORIA

after Sappho

The committee met on the first of the month to decide once and for all which of this black planet's myriad sights most honours the bold, high peaks of the human heart. A young man brought down his fist with a thud. There is nothing in this world, he cried, more stirring to the soul than a good parade! Sun striking the trumpets, the flash of batons, wind licking the flags into blazing bright sails. . . . Just then a fleet of gold jets roared past the high window in tight formation. Everyone looked up and gasped, stars in their eyes, and seemed on the point of consensus. A frail old man in a pale grey suit and matching cravat cleared his throat. Slow ripples moved through the room as he spoke, firmly, and not without eloquence, on behalf of the twin Spanish replica tall ships that had sailed that spring into harbour, bringing sailors and replica guns, firing replica cannons into the salt-sweetened air each evening at nine o'clock sharp. Some smiled to themselves and looked at their hands, some gingerly closed their reports, leaned forward in their seats and eyed the heavy wooden gavel in the chairman's hand. But I, who had been listening at the door for some time, distracted from my task (as happens often, and for which I am often sternly rebuked), slipped down the dim hall and out into the night where I joined the parade that had swallowed you.

LOVE SONNET

Now you are old and mostly bald
riding an antique bicycle.
You are wearing a neckbrace
and your posture — because of the bicycle?
because of the rolling Bavarian
hills in the background? —
is comically upright, as is,
in a way, your facial expression
which is nonetheless gentle
and nonetheless reticent
as you weave and swerve jerkily
in decreasing rings on the cobblestones
on which I am standing
remote   and also too close

INTRO TO LIT

I am ushered down the hall into a room
much like this one.
Should I close the door?
Should I take a seat?
There is no one to instruct me.
My guide has vanished in a chalky cloud.
I close the door. I take a seat.
Outside the window they are burying the river
under heavy, wet nets.
They are heaping broken bottles in the cargo hold of a ship.
I sit still on my white bench and wait.
I wait through the evening.
I wait through the night.
It dawns on me that perhaps you are not coming.
You, with your clipboard and your bandaged wing.
I see I will have to explain myself to myself.

PAST IMPERFECT

I was wearing my favourite hat.
I was crouching on a log.
I was breathing hard through a straw.
Ants were milking aphids on a leaf
and telescopes were tracking the soupy trails of stars.
The precincts were sleeping
while smoke cast a dazzling shadow
on the boathouse wall.
I was waiting for the day to arrange itself.
Carving names on a stick.
My family was waving from the deck of a ship
while a white dog paddled in its wake.
I was hoping to change things by staying the same.

THE VIEW

A plane touches down like a tiny red insect on the far side of a pair of binoculars. People disembark and the simile abruptly falls apart. According to certain laws of theoretical physics, it is possible I am not myself, but some "long dead" historical figure. But when I try to remember the future I keep getting stuck at 10:07 a.m. It is 10:07 a.m. The people stand around on the dock in little clusters, collecting their luggage, shielding their eyes from the sun. With every minute, each is moving towards a fading x pencilled in somewhere on a map. I feel certain I could find it if only I knew where to look. But there are clouds in the sky, small ones, and larger ones made of birds that rise and settle on the lakeshore between us. Soon it will be time to put on my shoes and go in. In the distance, high on the ridge, the blue lip of a glacier is quivering infinitesimally, on the brink, as it were, of breaking down. I can't see past it.

MARINER

Sometimes I eat an orange and completely forget about dying. Nonetheless, the thought of home can reliably be said to bring tears to the eyes of any traveller. When the sailor travels inland, he misses not so much the sight of the ocean as the sound it makes beneath him at night when the world has disappeared and there are only stars above to guide him. Perhaps he also misses the smell of creosote in the breeze, but it remains so utterly abstract in its absence he cannot properly be said to *feel* the lack. On the other hand, I find it possible to miss what I have never known. My voice has been described as nondescript, yet I continue to use it. I call to the hills and to the good people in them. I call to hear the sound of my own voice. The truth is, I seldom think about home at all. To grow up at sea is a mixed blessing, granted, but show me a blessing that isn't.

NOTES

The title "Lacrimae Rerum" is from Virgil's *Aeneid* (I. 462) and means "tears for things."

Sir Gromore Somyr Joure is one of the lesser-known knights of the Round Table in Sir Thomas Malory's *Morte Darthur*. The name appears variously in different editions (as Sir Gromoreson in the Winchester manuscript, for example); I have taken this spelling from the Caxton edition.

"Happiness Is Not the Only Happiness" takes its title from a line in James Richardson's *Vectors: Aphorisms and Ten-Second Essays* (Ausable Press, 2001).

The poem "Anaktoria" is an extremely loose translation of Sappho's Fragment 16.

ACKNOWLEDGEMENTS

Grateful acknowledgement is made to the editors of the following publications in which these poems first appeared, some in earlier versions: *Books in Canada*: "Sweet Basil"; *The Canary*: "Anaktoria"; *Court Green*: "And Also the Pleiades," "In Which All Will Be Revealed," "In Broad Daylight"; *The Denver Quarterly*: "Best-Case Scenario," "The View"; *Matrix*: "Before Darkness," "The Bridge," "Life with Folded Umbrella," "Shapes at Midnight," "The Starfish"; *Poetry*: "Dear Future"; and *Prairie Schooner*: "The Garden (I)," "The Garden (II)."

"Before Darkness," "The Garden (I)," "The Garden (II)," "The Onset," "Shapes at Midnight," and "What Is Called Déjà Vu" were published in the anthology *Breaking the Surface*, edited by Marilyn Bowering, Lorna Crozier, Susan Musgrave, Linda Rogers, and Patricia Young (Sono Nis, 2000).

"Another Bildungsroman" was published as a broadside in a limited edition by Delirium Press, Montreal, in 2002.

My thanks to the Canada Council for the Arts and to the Conseil des arts et des lettres du Québec for grants that supported me during the writing of this book, to Ray and Françoise LeBlanc, for so generously hosting me throughout the winter of 2001, to Heather McHugh, for her astute editorial advice, and to everyone at Anansi.

To my family, teachers, and friends, thank you for the difference in me.